T0128266

Galleon Moon

Galleon Moon
Puzzle Book

A collection of untitled poetry

By Frank Schroeder

GALLEON MOON
PUZZLE BOOK

iUniverse books may be ordered through booksellers or by contacting:

iUniverse
1663 Liberty Drive
Bloomington, IN 47403
www.iuniverse.com
1-800-Authors (1-800-288-4677)

Because of the dynamic nature of the Internet, any web addresses or links contained in this book may have changed since publication and may no longer be valid. The views expressed in this work are solely those of the author and do not necessarily reflect the views of the publisher, and the publisher hereby disclaims any responsibility for them.

Any people depicted in stock imagery provided by Thinkstock are models, and such images are being used for illustrative purposes only. Certain stock imagery © Thinkstock.

ISBN: 978-1-4917-8636-9 (sc)
ISBN: 978-1-4917-8637-6 (e)

Print information available on the last page.

iUniverse rev. date: 12/22/2015

You are about to embark on an odyssey of
the imagination, so come on board and
take your station as we explore new
poetic worlds.
Like the early 14th century explorer discovered
new lands and claimed them in honor, so
shall you, the reader, have
the same opportunity.
These untitled poems have spaces for you to
write in what you think is a good title.
If those were your poems what would YOU
name it?
Like history's early explorer's there are
even hidden treasures to find, interspersed
far left of the pages, of poems
So explore these poems often and soon as
you sail the stars of the Galleon Moon!

FLAPPING BUTTERFLYS

Flitting up above a mound
Lovely colors on wings abound
At a moment on a flower a lit
Perhaps for only a moment to sit
Patient, calmly on a dewy flower
In this moment, in this hour
Nothing in all of natures' beauty
Gravitates it from its duty
Blending in a bluish sky, I often
Utter, "why, oh why"?
To ask a question, "what keeps you calm"?
To watch, relaxes me like a balm
Each day I watch in infatuation
Rest you bring and relaxation
For a moment, your wings unfurled
Lets' me be in a calmer world
You I thank as you flap goodbye
So adieu my friend, you and I

Throbbing organ, oft I wonder
hopping up and down, over and
under, pulsating in
melodic rhyming
Pumping beats
in perfect timing
nary a miss in harmony
Giving life to you and me
how I'm thankful for its' play
Every second, minute, hour and day
All my life is like a flower prayer
Rest assured you'll always care
Thank you always that you're there

Just a hot summer day
Up jumps four legs, perhaps to play
Maybe to leap to catch a fly or
Perhaps for some shade to lie
I rest assured it will live
No reason to take its life but give
Gracious we all should be
Freedom for our right to be free
Rest assured for this nation and
Occasion, let's hop to this event.
Grateful for veterans for whom lives spent
Salute America independent!

Ebony tusk white as snow
Lushly foraging on African plains
Ecological climates reduce the rains
Poaching tusks of ivory
How long until we see their pleas
And do we need more piano keys?
Now they speak with sub sonic flair
Travel on ground faster than sound in air
So treat with respect to show we care

Lurching in jungles the king of beasts
Infinitely searching for some feasts
Often pouncing on antelope and more
Now king of the jungle, hear it ROAR

Calypso dancing in a carnival town
Aruba, Jamaica where I can be found
Regally clad in carnival wear
Island dancing on the square
Barbados is beautiful under a
Blue sapphire sky
Enjoying the beach with a mai tai
Antilles calm winds under a bright moon
Not wishing to leave but be back soon

Wafting winds carry and spar
Into air near and far
Nearing nests to trees and aeries
Ground below it feels so freed
Small creatures below revere its' need

Mostly considered ancestors of the
Everyday domestic dog from
Xalpa, these trusted
Instinctive hunters and
Canines
Are not to be (trusted but feared).
Nothing could be further from the truth
Great parents but a
Rarity in state
Extermination is their fate
Yet we can step in (before it's too late).
Wise, powerful hunters can follow scents,
Odors of prey a mile or so away
Lone hunters in the midst
Very few (only 60) still
Exist
Such a pity to see these species desist

Hollowing out burrows with rodent like teeth and claws
Ambly backwards digging with rarely a pause
Inconvenient fences are merely dug under
Rarely seen but often a plunder
You may think that they be slow and tire
No, they can run twenty five mile an hour
Often keeping that speed for ninety seconds
Startled, they charge humans and "bowl em" down
Edge sharp teeth bite through a rubber boot,
Diving into a tunnel, use donkey kicks to elude
With powerful sharp badger like teeth and claws
Often will protect itself, given the cause
Muscular marsupials, once were many to date
But cattle grazing, dingos reduced them to 138
And I must not forget its' main enemy
Tasmanian devils they scurry and flee
So lets' use our rumps to keep them free.

At feet size twelve inches wide
Few of these animals are awkward in stride
Reaching heights of nineteen feet tall
It's not very awkward at all
Chewing with tongues of twenty two inch
And reaching most leaves is a cinch
Now able to reach in its' power
Galloping speeds thirty seven miles an hour
In the wild it loves to play
Rarely sleeping (three minutes a day)
At nineteen feet tall gives a good view
For hungry lions who want to eat you
Fun facts I hope you encircle and shine
Enjoy this puzzle and facts of mine

Armored with bands of bone and armor
Reaching 130 pounds, it's a charmer
Meandering with a twenty inch tail
Agility in burrows it does impale
Digging deeply into dirt
Its' large, powerful claws it will exert.
Longating itself into a round ball
Locking itself into a spare
Or bowling anyone? Anywhere?

Blues sadly fill the air
Reeking low with despair
Overcome with such emotion
Keeping in my heart a notion
Eventually things will get better
Nothing but time will loosen these letters

Rather heavy (7,700 pounds) and rather big (twelve-
feet long)
Horns can reach up as a three foot tall prong
If can charge thirty five miles an hour if the need
Nourishing on lush African reed
Of armor two inches thick
Chewing leaves is their trick
Ebony tusks and horns they are poached
Rile not this animal, it will rage
Or go on a short burst rampage
So leave it be and do not encroach

Catch a glimpse of the brightest hue
Royal red through and through
Infinite bright in its' wisdom
More majestic than any kingdom
Soft and subtle as the cardinal
Other colors are merely marginal
Next to an apple a redbird sings
Sweet and broken a red sunset wanes

Bent shaped horn on its' noggin
Lets' you pass by and that's a bargain
Aggressive if it feels the need
Can you run at thirty miles per hour?
Know it can and has the power.
Rambling on nettles
Hungry to crunch
In a hurry
No time to munch
Oh be careful when you're around
Caution when you near its' mound
Easily with tons of power
Rages at you at thirty miles per hour
One tail, four feet, twelve toes, "nuff said"
See what grows on top of its' head?

Hungry is an
Understatement.
Munching down two thousand to nine thousand
Pounds of fish a day is
Barely a bite of food or snack on
A tray.
Capable of living ninety five years young
Keeping trim and fit isn't much fun
Weighing in at sixty five tons
Highly intelligent as they make "songs"
And harmonize in a good "sing-a-longs"
Let's keep them safe, come what may
Eating eight thousand pounds of "burp" fish a day

Misty evenings you come in sight
Over eons you rise in flight
Oh youthful face watch us each night
Nestle our pillows ever so slight

Methuselah generation I have no gripes with
Orange wings and black stripes
Nearly each
Autumn brings these flitters flapping
Rearing it's young like
Children tapping
Hopping three thousand miles from Canada to Mexico
Breeding seven to eight months or so
Unlike their parents who only live weeks
This is like having children
That live five hundred years at its' peak
Eight months surviving, like being immortal
Revolving through life (like a time portal.).
Flight planning (three months before winter)
Larvae, then pupa, then caterpillars.
You see emerge beautiful, but foul tasting
Sol the pattern means. "Your time you'd be wasting!"

True beauty is not in pride
Hidden not in private but
Enshrining inside
Bursting with wisdom, it is our wealth
Experience of life, of ills, of health
A diary of life, it is our flower
Utter triumph we can empower
The soul is the essence of who we are
You must enjoyably bear this duty
Within yourself deep is this beauty
Inside your soul is an eternal fountain
That quenches your thirst, come any mountain
Hidden inside, not on the surface
It will arise when you call its' purpose
No, it will empower when you call its' hour

Cotton candy floating
Under a clear blue sky
Much like a coating
Up one thousand feet high
Lofting like a rounded tower
Upward they spread
Similar looking as a
Cauliflower
Looming above the earth in
Ominous power
Upward they reach, dark and lorn
Developing into a thunderstorm
So what images do you see in hidden form?

Lifting thoughts linger in your mind
Often as sails to fill your dreams
Vessel of hope catching breeze and wind
Each whispering voice carrying you out to sea it seems

Columning up, ply by ply
Underneath a sapphire sky
Musrooming anvil over rivers and lakes
Utter respect is what it takes
Ladden with rain, lightning and hail
Often called a "super cell"
Nestling alone or in a clusters
Indeed these are "picnic busters"
Massive-cold air serves its purpose as
Buoyant warm air begins to surface
Upward with a colliding cold motion
Summer creates rainstorms and in winter snow
Climbing has no where else to go
Lightning, moisture, warm unstable air
Of energy rising to lift it somewhere
Ushering rain, lightning, wind and thunder
Demonstrating the awe of natures wonder
So hold your ears as it claps asunder!

Smart enough, I know it's me
Easy to stay, not run and flee
Lest to say winners stand their ground
Fearless when trouble comes around
Easily you <u>are</u> good enough
Smart ones don't quit when times get tough
Team up with another with strength and pride
Even a bully will step aside
Even add three friends or maybe four
Make your stand strong, they'll bully no more

Gliding moments setting
Reverence of blessings
Admission for divine assistance
Courteous time for non-resistance
Ease of movement in body and heart
Shall we be thankful of this we impart

Must believe <u>I AM</u> good enough
And agile when times are rough
Relying on myself I am willing to try
To not trust "quitting" as an alibi
I am smart, strong, able and wise
And won't use failures as alibis
Long I see drugs as an excuse
Alcohol, addiction, such abuse
Rather I see something better
Tae kwan do, karate, judo, scrimmage
Strengthens my body, mind and image

Seeking comfort for my soul
Often I don't know where to go
Lift me up, I'm sinking down
And I don't know where the answer found
Comfort, console me and empower
Ease my heart this day and hour

Wistful dreams of days gone by
Hovering glow of fireflies
In the grass with four leaf clovers
So wishing such days will ne'er be over
Perhaps in an orchard picking a peach
Effortlessly jumping for those out of reach
Relaxing in a hammock, getting a tan
Iced tea in one hand, the other a fan
Nearby orange breasted robins are chirpping
Glass of crushed ice with a straw I'm slurping
Contentment and peace I wish to mold
Asking all worries just put "on hold"
Lulling in a gentle, soft blowing breeze
Mulling the moment when all is at ease

Try not to worry of things you can't sway
Everyone takes life like a big drama play
Addressing the issues, crying the blues
Racing with tissues, you can't see the hues
Sobbing and crying won't ease the pain
On-twenty four hours past will return again
Feeling blues day long will drive you insane
Stead watch the stars twinkle and gleam
Try dare to dream of impossible dreams
Attempt to be more than what you are
Reach within you with all of your might
Light up your confidence like a star at night
Inside is strength and optimistic power
Growing inside of you every hour
Have you seen the stars glowing so bright?
Then I think its' time you do. (Starting tonight)!

No amount of peace building will be able to last
Accept each as equals, not live in the past
The most humble people that you are among
Usher in hope, harmony and song
Ring in harmony in a soft silence
Ending societies call to violence
Societies ignorance to those in need
Bandage those in poverty bleed
Effortlessly society pushes to this margin
And loses a part of itself in the bargain
Untill we do this, nothing will change
Then give a stranger a friendly smile and hello
You'd be surprised how far it can go

Ask me what I'm feeling as
My mind begins to melt
I can't hold back from reeling
To this pulse that starts to swell
Her eyes and arms, her legs and
Ears won't comfort your disease
Only you can look inside your heart
Now is the time and place to start.
Linger on? Do I belong?
You must ask face to face
On my emotion are you feeling?
Not just here as I wither bleeding
Embrace me! Not just "come hither"

Lip stain red is its' color
Only drained it reaches its' pallor
Vanished is its' bright red hue
Embracing you with all my grips
Lingering to your lasting lips
It's hard not hearing but talk abounds
Echoes are spearing with piercing sounds
Silence is golden, your beauty divine
Blest as I'm holding your hand in mine
Looking as your hair carresses your face
Ecstatic like heaven has reserved this place
Embracing you gives no greater glee
Draining and waning, ebbing inside
I know no greater truth I can hide
Never before as I have no doubt
Giving you love is what blessings about

Jumping through the cosmic sky
Undulating like a fire fly
Pouring like raindrops in a hot summer rain
Intimately cooling the skin of its' pain
To every season comes consolation
Everyone peace and obligation
Rainbows paint colorful bows like those
Face painters paint on your cheek and nose
And can you remember sandcastles you've made?
Lugging umbrellas for protection and shade?
Like Jupiters' stars and grains of sand
It's given the task to each woman and man
Now is the time for peace and for strength
God grant me a ruler to measure its length

Marathon planet in speed will disperse
Easily known god of travel and commerce
Racing along with such hasty speed
Could be the wings on the balls of its feet
Ushering along in outer space
Reeling along with dignity and grace
You ever wonder, sooner or later
Revealing water in protected craters
It closely resembles the moons landscape
Such moon dentations you can not escape
Its high quality image from mariner ten
Noting planet vulcan may be its' twin
Given an answer more easier to see
Science Einsteins Theory of relativity

I'm sometimes down and oh so weary
And find myself sad and my eyes teary
Mountains are just mere boulders to me
Reaching up to you I dust off my shoulders
And there is no life without hunger pains
I can't run the ball with no yardage gains
Such boulders ahead are merely a stone
Every sea has its' waves that don't wash alone
Drawing my strength on staffs and staves
Up I will stand on this stormy sea
Positive to walk strong to all I can be

Quench my thirst, ease my mind
Upon this hunt where I must find
Every step I must embark
Search the covenant for my arc hidden
Then ends my hunt, my treasure embedden

Sixth planet from the sun of its berth
Average radius is nine times of earth
Though one eigth earths density impressive
Upon volume is ninety five times more massive
Rings around Saturn are ice, rocks and dust
Nine rings continuously floating like crust
Sixty two moons orbit (fifty three are named)
Electro magnetic fields are to blame
Titan, its' moon is awesome and weird
The only moon with substantial atmosphere
Imagine wind speeds eleven hundred miles an hour
Neptunes winds no where near that power
Giant titan, Saturns rings, what a scoop!
Shooting through a colorful basketball hoop

The silence fills these empty walls
Here the guilt of my conscience calls
Edging up to make its claim
Cleansing me of guilt and shame
Oh to rid myself of pain and sorrow
Niching in my bones and marrow
Firmly setting into my mind
Etched in life by the hands of time
Silently I sit in a pew
So wishing to clear and start anew
I sit staring at a sheer mesh skin
Oh, bless me father for I have sinned
No I recall not when I came here lost
Anxious with penance my sins to toss
Lord tell me what is the cost?
Well there's no mortgage or loan to be made
In Christs' death they have been paid
Now accept him deep in your heart
Delivered, I absolve you, my blessings impart
Obey him totally in heart and in mind
Worry not, but seek good and live
Such unexplainable rewards in heaven he shall give

The space craft hovers over a lunar heaven
Here in the capsule of Apollo eleven
Eagle here, we copy you down"
Momentarily they will be on the ground
Oh such a good spot o'er that crater landing
One hundred feet, slow, slow handling
Now one hundred feet, fuel five percent
Fingers crossed on this descent
Remaining fuel is five percent
On my feet while in motion
My prayers are with you and emotions
Then seventy five feet and good looking
Here my body and nerves are snookin
Energy fuel sixty seconds to go
Ere the call of "bingo!"
And now just thirty seconds of fuel left
Raising a footprint, salute and our flag
The mission is over Neil Armstrong commanded
Houston, tranquility base, the eagle has landed"
                              April 20, 1969

Vibrant at night as the evening star
Each venutian day lasts 3,800 hours
Notably an earth day of seventy degrees
Upon Venus is eight hundred seventy three
Such on a hellish land to have dwelt
Roasts hot enough to make lead melt
Inhaling carbon dioxide is such a pain
Sulphor cloud acids falling like rain
Intense heat would boil water away
Noting a basketball a ten foot dunk ease
Goes as a eleven foot dunk is a breeze

Whirl like the wind
At a three beat measure
Leading and swirling
Tempo and pleasure
Zig and zag your partner you treasure

Detail in fill an awe stunning light
Each people... flowers... angels delight
Such hearts stand in exhillerance shining
Can you feel its brilliance binding?
Restful people, their inner self calmed
Infused their needs sated, happy and balmed
People are of same age about thirty two
Treading against a deep sky of sapphire blue
I-trust in his love to attain this mending
Of surrender my past to his tending
Now I bask in ecstatic elation
Of colors so rich they defy exclamation
Fiery hell exists, this I believe
Here imagine having shingles and no relief
Eternal love, small angels above you
And surrounded by friends past and present that love you
Vivid colors aura lee arrayed
Even Picasso, Matisse or Renoir
Never such artists have ever displayed
Say now you accept him, in this Ive prayed

Hiding emotions long dwelling inside
Isolated to trust someone to confide
Dare shall I live in a shadow so bleak?
Dare shall they judge me as someone weak?
Every strength I have within my soul
Now goes at length for one common goal
Freedom to be the person I can be
Escaping the doubts of desparity
Encouragement, confidence, I know I can win!
Leaning on my power comes from within
I will not let anyone change my direction
No, my compass needle is my selection
Go north or south or east or west
Soul searching inside for which way is best

Fishing on a home made raft
Leaning gently fore and aft
Over the water you gently glide
As you lay all your worries to the side
To hear the paddles softly splashing
Idling forward by boats you are passing
Nearing closely by those on the bank
Graciously waving to your right flank
On a breeze filled day you have no needs
Notice ducks swimming nestled in reeds
Anticipate not on problems and woes
Slosh gently the river of life where ever it goes
Troddling the stream won't make you go faster
Relax in ease the pressure you'll master
Every lifes journey has beauty so scenic
Ambling through speedily just makes you anemic
Majestic peace he will deliver
So eeeze back and enjoy your ride upriver

Can you go on a s-p-a-c-e j-o-g with the colors of heavens city walls?

Jade

Sapphire

Agate

Emerald

Chrysolite

Granite

pearl

Onyx

Spell s-p-a-c-e j-o-g in an anagram (here is an example to get you started)

1. Sapphire

2. Pearl

3.

4.

5.

6.

7.

8.

There are moments in life
When all you can feel
Is you miss
Someone you dream of so much
That you could reach out and hold them for real
Some days I have those moments, more
Often I find
Funneling through my memories
Caponing like a mountain climb
Or wanting to rest on a narrow ledge
Notching and knuckling for a finger wedge
Sometimes I sit for a moment to ponder
Clearing a while the pressure I'm under
I bask in the sunset of a beautiful show
Escorting the orange ball yond a plateau
Now I'm at peace, my blood pressure lower
Calmness I seek as the orange ball glowers
Ending my pangs like a soft soothing salve
Serenity exists in the comfort I have

Silently moving like the glow of a candle
Oh Lord I'm blessed with so much to handle
Finitely tiny grasping my finger
This unexplainable joy I wish to linger
Cherub from heaven I hold in my arms
Holding this bundle with all of its charms
I feel its skin like velvet and pure
Labor nine months and this does occur
Delivery over, a healthy young child
Obsessed with emotions, it's calm but mild
Fame or fortune, poor or wealthy
Matters not here as long as its healthy
In soon time grade school, high school and college
Nesting memories, knowledge and love
Enrapture smooth blessings given from above

Secluded alone by a rippling stream
Often I'll relax, sit and dream
Lolling by a lazy river
Isolate, alone of my own endeavor
Transformed away from bustle and frills
Under the trees and whipporwills
Detached from others for a while
Enjoying time of being alone
Off from a place of traffic cones
Frequenting a silence of restful sound
Pleasurable orchestra of crickets abound
Easing back by a tranquil stream
Anxiety lowers and blood pressure it seems
Calmness relieves a body adrift
Enjoying ones leisure is a special gift

Transform yourself to your past
Happiness you thought would ever last
Reaching for a tire swing
Or a favorite toy was your thing
Underneath a blanket sheet
Giving yourself a private retreat
Having a whack with a baseball bat
And wiping your feet on the doorstep mat
Casting a line with a hook and worm
How that bait would wiggle and squirm
Innocence was love and grace
Like a puppy licking you in the face
Driving a toy tractor you were a farmer
Sitting by a winter fire to get warmer
Each winter sledding down a snow hill
You warm with hot cocoa to relieve chill
Each night your forehead is kist from above
Somehow you knew you were blest with love

Awesome waterfall colors and glows
Under natures amazing light shows
Reactive charged particles with magnetic power
Oncome and collide with earths atmo shower
Radiant plus energy expressed as light
Awe struck, this is a beautiful sight!
Burning sun causes hydrogen/helium to fuse and race
Our proton electrons are shot into space
Running particles then speed and shower
Energizing us with solar wind power
As the earth magnetic lines draw particles surge
Lines of magnetic poles then will converge
Ionosphe gas atoms collide and lights will glow
Such is created a beautiful light show
Northern lights in the sky you spied
It depends on the gas particles that collide
Green and dark red are oxygen atoms
Hues of purple as a rule are nitrogen molecules
The other colors pink and light yellow
Sunsets make colors look subtle and mellow
Discovering this beauty exciting and new
Awaits an experience for me and you
Waterfalls of shifting colors and hues
Nitrogen bits of sharp blues bid you adieu

Harps aloft strum in praising
Angelic chords with voices raising
Lifting up a heavenly choir
Lancing you with heart felt fire
Each one with their beckoning calls
Like major lifts and minor falls
Uniting voices gainst heavens walls
Justice was blind but proof was strong
Amend the rights, correct the wrong
Heaven holds a place for those who belong
A feeling that I've recalled before
Like I have previously walked this floor
Lingering in an ancient past
Echoing "The die is cast!"
Love is not a victory
Unless his blood's shed for you and me
It's a call which we must respond
Above it all, far and beyond

Zurrender your inner body and mind
Enter into a personal quiet time
Nature calls to close your eyes
Time alone with peace and calm
Resting with "Ahs, ooohs and aaahms"
Abdomen breathe for just two minutes
Nuture and focus air entering infinite
Quiet and calm, your lungs' air is a sail
Undulating rythym, inhale and exhale
Inside deep, soft, subtle, vibrant hues
Lulls your mind in purrfect catlike mews
Inner qualms laid while soft music plays
Then allaying all your worries away
You're in your "safe place" while you are here
This is a place of no worries or fears.
It's laying in a field of fresh smelling clover
Melting your worries like an April fresh rain
Easing you back to present moment again.

Easing back in your favorite chair
As you slowly inhale the air
Resting back, exhale out slow
Tenderly relieve your mind of woe
Horizons await you with each new day
Slowly let your cares just drift away
Mental feel each "om om om" mantra
Ooozing worries with each new chantra
Kniving away like a knife into smoke
Ease blood pressure when you evoke
Find soft music, tranquil and private
Island breezes await when you arrive at
Renew your soul, body and mind
Escape just a moment with your worries behind

Drifting high as a cloud on sails
Aloft I fly over hills and vales
Flitting lands a butterfly
Flashing its' colors against the sky
Off in a distance hummingbirds hums
Droning a beat like distant drums
In this field I'll lie often
Lifting, lacing to my skin softened
Laying in this Eden of solitude
Dreaming in a vacant pensive mood
Along mossy stones and willows
Nestling white petals on rocks as pillows
Clouds cross over as soft winds enhance
Escort each flower to this dance
Reeling in natures' beauty spewed
Sated earths' spotless flaw of quiet solitude

(Curious fact)
Daffodill bulbs produce galantamine.
A drug commercially used to combat
Alzheimers, it is an alkaloid derived from the-bul
(Also known as razadyne, nivalin and lycoremine).

Across vast acres of tan tossed wheat
My America ev'ry morning I'll meet and greet
Barley stretches far and wide
Etched across the country side
Rocks and forests, seasides and plains
Won by veterans blood and pains
All too often, all too long
Veterans penned this freedom song
Eye in awe this richness intaken
So they who have died will not be forsaken
From the temples and wooded lands
Let all reach out, hand in hand
Our flag of stars still waves unfurled
With strength, peace and right secured.

To which no beginning to which no end
Immortal expanses to alter and bend
Memories we can escape to that day
Enveloped in dreams to take me away
Looking at endless faces and names
Everlasting, eternal as gaslit flames
Securing a hope for peace and change
Sating to lope, it is us! We must arrange!
Desires that create an inspiration
Reposing the mind in true affirmation
Each vision lasts twenty minutes (less if you snore)
Average visions are three to five a night (or more)
Magical, mystical, adventurous schemes
Softly whispering to a much calmer being.

Drift down the aisle and take a seat
Rest your head, your back, your feet
Ease on back, be spoiled and pampered
A drift your mind in peace unhampered
Music to lull, relax and calm
Just take it in like a massaging balm
Our porters prepare a soothing foot spa
Under softh cashmere towels you will "ooh!" and "aaah!"
Release from cares, your comfort is here
No worries or concerns, just soft cashmere
Enjoy a meal from our home cooked buffet
You deserve to be pampered, coddled and swayed
Soft hands massage your neck and back
Take in the pleasure, nothing to lack
Attendees cater to your every desire
Tucking your pillow when you tire
It has been I hope an enjoyable ride
Our hope for some moments you feel better inside
Now in peace and love we hope you abide

Whittling deeper than wetness can forge
Abrasive erosion creates a deep gorge
Tears to me are often like this
Edging my face like a windblown mist
Racing along ridges and tiers
Falling like angel falls are my tears
Accumulating and dropping over a river stream
Landsliding into a field of dreams
Laser-like cutting hard rock into soft
Deeply raising my visions aloft
Rapidly now plunging into Edens' pool
Escaping this, I'd be a fool
And no doubt will I forego this pleasure
Mustn't deny myself of this timeless treasure

Randomly floating out to sea
Endless tides carry me
Easing back in eternal motion
Following the sway of a distant ocean
Dreams abound as I sway
Restful sounds of an ocean spray
I lay quiet in a hynotic trance
Flirting in tides that invite me to dance
Taking their hand I bow and accept
I curtsy and dance to their heights and depths
Nudging me gently I softly awaken
God speed my friend to the dance I have taken

Now is the period tween dusk and dawn
Illuminate of day is now gone
Give way to evening as the red sun lows
Hoot owls sing as wise moon glows
Troubles ease as calmness now flows

There are moments in life
When all you can feel
Is you miss
Some one you dream of so much
That you pick them out and hold them for real
Some days I have those moments more
Often I-find
Funneling through my memories
Caponing like a mountain climb
Or I wanting to rest on a narrow ledge
Notching and knuckling for a finger wedge
Somtimes I sit for memories to ponder
Clearing a while the pressures I'm under
I bask in the sunset of a-beautiful show
Escorting the orange ball beyond a plateau
So often in life I've basked and glowered
Now I'm at peace, my blood pressure lowered
Calmness I seek like a dawn/new flower
Ending my pang like a soft soothing salve
Serenity exists in-the comfort I have

Huddling
Under a
Mess of clothes lies
A package of sinew and bones
Neatly stacked like a package
Fresh in form
I often who prepares-it
Grave I'm informed soon declares it
Utter folly to deny
Resolute, I must try to
Enjoy this package till I die

Gray forms pale
Haunts my soul like an
Ominous spectre of a life long past
Scurry around my consciousness like a
Thief stealing prescious memories

Infinity, for
Man to live 3/4 a century
Must surely be reward enough but
Oh contraire, why shouldn't this
Red blooded sun
Tanned, cancered form be
Around for years longer?
Living man
Inflates himself. I will stretch
Trut and tight my
Years. In the end, we will know.

Not a flash or a flicker or slimmer of light
In a cleft of clouds this moonless night
Girdling above silently brightens
Heavens giant Orion tightens, the dreams of mans-helms
The beauty of space and uncharted realms

Timeless expansion and contraction like a
Heart beating in the
Endless throbs of space
Blatantly, it
Invades galaxies, moons and nebulae
Galactic lungs
Breathe incessantly for eons beyond time
And explode in the unrestrained spheres of space
No wonder God's celestial fireworks
Gather our eyes heavenward
To the extreme limits of our earthly eyesight
Here is an explosion of
Energies
Others pale in comparsion
Rythymic beating of pulsars and black holes
Yin and yang bing and BANG

Colorful horses orbit as children scream
Among bottle toss, balloon burst and ice cream
Rotating rainbow saddles
Oncoming-children grab head bridles
Under bright blue cotton puff skies
Silly clowns play with whipped cream pies
Errant balloons from children flies and
Levitates from a sad childs' eyes

Under a white thumbnail moon
Night will be giving away soon to
Immediate morning
Coming like a thief, no notice
Or warning
Rising along a songbirds sing
Nestling one horn on its' head
Spiraling spikes specially bred

Drawing fire flaming heat
Reptiles with claws on feet
Ancient beasts of medieval times
Gracing shields and English steins
Often seen with wings in flight in air
Now I like mine medium rare!

Guardians of the forest world
Narly dwarfs with feet a curled
Often mixing brews, gathering seeds
Ministering to medicinal needs
Eighteen inches tall in miniature tree homes
Such is the end of my gnome poem

Energetic, fun loving, mischievous/folks
Loves to play practical-jokes
Venturing with magical powers
Everyday haunting woods and towers
So if hiking be good, if you're in their neighborhood

Black as obsidian, stars
Emigrate to their assigned positions, each
And every one standing at attention
Under the watchful eye of their heavenly maker.
The enormous moon hangs low over the horizon,
Yellow as a Kansas sunflower. In a
Hundred years from now someone may see
All these things.
Soon, perhaps, there will be colonists on the
Moon and someone will write this poem;
Early yesterday morning the earth hung low on
A lonely horizon hill. Two lovers wait till
Night for a beautiful earth light rendezvous.
I will see these things here, but somewhere, like a
Night heron winging toward dawn, I will
Gather in flight to the early morn.

Stones have stood the eons of time, the
Titans of eternity. These defiers of
Oblivion for ages lay
Nondescript in the landscape. Since
Earth was formed man has all but
Chiseled out his meager existence bearing
Upon himself a lasting
Tribute --- yet for countless
Thousands of years they've stood
Eternity will end, the sun blacken and die
Rocks will cleft for ages to come.

Crushed and down, I am so tired
Heavy weight, this my burden be
Each day I wait by you inspired
Raised by your hand, I can cross any sea
I find-the path across lifes' mountains
Strong 'to drink tears from its' watery fountains
How I thank you, a rock, that I can count on

Hearty flung fires
Ashes embers glow
Reddish embers
Dart to and fro
Wide awake
Open eyed
Open flames
Deep and dried
Finely laid
Lacquered lillies
Oiled and waxed
Oh, how the smiles
Really shine
Sleeping on this floor of mine

Fleeting glimpses of granite shoreline dart
Out tween mists of heavy green pines
Greening like missiles shot into space
Breaking like thistles on a shrub face
Out in the shadows boat motors hum
A throbbing of engines, closer they come
Then soon I see them a stones throw away
Soon they will lead me safe back to the bay

Counting the hours and days
Occupying my mind
Moment to moment to see your face
Entangled in your arms entwined
How I wait to walk with you
Oh so much, I'm burdened
My long awaited reunion too
Ease my heart, I love you for certain

Reddish beauty
Often it grows
Sunset heighten its
Elegant glows
Bedded in gardens
Luster in grace
Often put in a flower vase
Ooh! In true beauty and color afire
Moment awaiting my true loves desire

Vibrant elation, we have won
I will sing success in this song
Celebrate, we have prevailed
The enemy has poorly failed
Opponents have no power
Rejoice with me in our finest hour
Your triumph is sweet, their defeat sour

Poetic Secret Surprise Tales (PSST)!

I walked upon a lonely hill since the break of dawn and looked to relieve my skin of chill and a rock to rest upon. A field mouse came up next to me, perhaps to just keep warm or perhaps to keep itself safe from any harm. I spied aloft, in half drowsed sleep, a huge and hungry hawk. Better not to make a peep, better not to talk. I lay frozen, not a word, the mouse still by my side. After fifteen minutes flew, bear bird, don't waste sun." "There is other food for you. Today we're not the ones." With these words he gave me a grin and winked an eye or two. And with a great draft of wind went off into the sky blue. I looked at the mouse and he at me. He placed his paw upon my knee. With a couple of squeaks and a toothy grin as if to say "Thank you my friend!" Then off he went into a matte of leaves and that's my story if you believe. That's my tale upon this rock. The strange tale of the mouse and the hawk.

Against a soft crystal-blue sky wind blown tufts-of clouds float by expanding like soft cotton balls. I sometime contemplate the cause of this laying barefoot in the bliss and caressing kiss of a soft light breeze mid singing birds and buzzing bees.

Quietly collecting natures pollen, natures timeless springtime-calling us to lay back and sniff the spring air, smell the roses.

The grass is greener somewhere else, man persuades and we comply and when we get to somewhere else we find the grass is dry. And when we look back behind us to see where we have been. We've found the best place we've just left is really, really green!

Black smoke puffs from a funnel smoke stack, the western star was on the tracks carrying logs goods and lamps, crossing a trestle near an Indian camp where Indian squaws make open fires and horseback warriors yell their desires by a fallen river stream. Near rushing waters elders dream by teepees of ancient days of watching eagles fly into the haze and hunting buffalo as they graze. Remember days a when they wore war bonnets and danced by the fire chanting Indian sonnets. Respecting the earth, moon and sun. Once there were many, now there are none. The Indian days have turned to night, what once was red has turned to white.

From the moment of your birth angels were at your side, shielding you from harm, wishing just to guide. They keep a vigil every day and touch your dreams at night. They comfort in your hour of need, regardless of the plight. So if you believe in angels, let them know you care. And when troubles come along, you'll know they'll be there!

Brandish fact as being true
Etched and latched inside of you
Locked deep inside as timeless lockets
Indelible depths and deep pockets
Engraved in the face of each expression
Vault of our most valuable possession
Expression of hope and intercession.

In the early dawn a pansy widens its petals in the morning rays. Sitting outside the window it watches as a family eats breakfast, reads stories and plays with the children and dog by the fire. Rooted in soil its sad eyes convey its longing. Oh! To be part of that warm loving family!," it sighs. Sniff! Sniff!, snip! Now the rootless pansy finds itself indoors staring out the window of the garden it was once in, staring out at the wide eyed pansies in the garden.

The cycle once again continues-
A pansy widens its petals outside in early mornin rays.

Things are now different, I cannot run with you in the sun or evenings, along the shore or in the park, no never more; remember how I would scratch on the door bringing in leaves or mud on the floor? Those familiar scratches to go in or out? And when you would scold me how my-brown eyes would pout. I cannot lie by the warm fire so red, or cozy up to you in the middle of bed. Or lie by feet to protect you from harm, or lie on your neck to keep you warm. Though I lie below you in six feet of ground, you must know the peace I have found, a peace more peaceful than I've ever known and hey, I must tell you I've found my old bone I buried so long ago. You were my master, but also my friend. I love you always, that will never end. I am not lonely. I have no fear. I love you only. You'll always be here.

Yesterday morning the sun hung low, rays warm the flowers in a basking glow. Yellow and round rose the warm dawn; birds chirp and fly in a diamond blue sky as puffy clouds sail. I don't know why each break-of day is more beautiful than the last. I know that the future of the whole human race from the very first dawn has felt this same sun on the break of their faces. And I bask in the glow of the knowledge redeeming. Like a beautiful dawn; forever, this beauty has meaning.

Home made apple pie
Butterflies in the fall
Crocuses in the spring
Babies when they crawl
Moonlight on a wooded lane
Eating a fresh ripe peach
Window boxes in full bloom
And a dream that's within reach
Childrens birthday parties
Fireflies in the yards
Living in your forties
When you win at cards
Pushing childrens on a swing
Having a heart-to-heart
Rainbows breaking from a storm
Sunsets at days end
Bedtime dogs to keep you warm
You may've thought there's no end
But I would save the best for last
And one last thing is true
That my most favorite thing of all
Is having a friend like you!!!

The old snake charmer raises his arms, sitting cross legged amid the swarms of people watching in the old market square. Anticipation cuts the air as flute music plays on. Suddenly but slowly, up from the basket emerges a black cobra snake his head to a melodic dance, head moving in waves like-some like some hypnotic trance. Obstinate reptile that stops its' ears, the voice of enchanters it may not hear casting its spells and cunning charms. It just moves with the flow of his masters' arms.

The Wedding Day

Hooves and wheels came ever nearer, up the old road
it becomes ever clearer. And old buckskin mare,
haggard and lank, plodding the ground along the
wet bank.
The face of the driver was pale and burned
out. His body was twisted as he fidgeted about;
Next to the seat lay a long halter, to lead the
mare in case it should salter.
The dog barked loudly as the lone woman
stood in the doorway near a rick of fresh wood.
Covering her shoulder with white shawl and hat
she enters the carriage in from the back;
"Hop in ma'am, we'll be on our way. Don't want
to be late on your wedding day."
"My congrats to you and new groom.
Sit back and relax there's plenty of room."
Slowly she stands and steps from the carriage,
"anticipating a beautiful marriage."
Walking the narrow aisles of the chapel; fears
and wonders too many to grapple.
There was a pleasant smell from the stable
that day. The scent of new straw and fresh cut hay,

music and laughter. Make no mistake, there's no
deception. It's going to be a beautiful reception.
The windows were done in a bright festive hue,
with heart shaped signs of "I love you."
"It is late and I must be going," softly she cried as
the people were showing up at the chapel. There
came her parents, neighbors and friends, flower girl,
bride's maids, those she depends on since she was
small
such good people, God bless them all."
Now up to drive, nearing the room," Land sakes
alive!
Here comes the groom, parents, friends and
the best man. "Can't see me yet." So as quick as
she can she's off to her room.
Now dressed in white, the music starts playing.
"Dearly beloved," the preacher starts saying. The
emotion
so thick you can cut with a knife. Finally it's
here. "You are now man and wife. You may now
kiss the bride." And with tears and with laughter.
comes our wishes anew. That you live happily
after too.

Across vast acres of tan tossed wheat
My America every morning greet
Barley stretches far and wide
Etched across the country side
Rocks and forests, seasides and plains
Won by veterans blood and pains
All too often and all too long
Veterans penned this freedom song
Eye in awe this richness intaken
So they who have died will not be forsaken
From the temples and wooded lands
Let's reach out hand to hand
Our flag of stars will wave unfurled
With strength and peace our freedom secured

Gray pale forms
Haunt my soul like an
Ominous specter of a life long past
Scurrying around my consciousness like a
Thief stealing precious memories

Oh pale and brittle pencils, to try
    To draw a grass blades curve against
The sky or one birds talons that clings to
    Limbs. Oh, cracked twilights mirrors ever to dim
Catch one rainbow color, one glinting flash of
    Beauty and awesome splendor of natures realm.
Consider the truth of what I've said
    Love the eyes that see, the mind that can wander
Love the music you hear, the wings of thunder

Sidewalks under maple trees laced in a
    August shaded breeze,
Cattle munch in clover fields as
    Fishermen bring in their daily yields.
Boys and girls stop their cars
    Feel the moon, touch the stars.
Quiet ring the flowers as
    Cat tails stand like sentry towers.
Hear the crickets in grass, frogs as they rigget.
    Remember our youth as we used to live it?
Go back and recall how it was.
    Remember man, for all of us.

Fragrant mists caress my cheeks in
    The blue hills of Kentucky.
I want to feel that mountain breeze of
    Which I'd feel so lucky.
To see the crest of a silver moon
    Rise against the timberline
To feel the whisp of swaying trees
    And its' scent of pine
To watch towboats chug down river
    Next to Louisvilles river bank
To watch a cardinal as they deliver
    Oh, so much to thank.
To feel the serenity of peace
    Upon a lovely hill
Such as when you win at cards
    And when a wildcat screams
Such I dream of blessings like these
    And I always will it seems.

Sweeping across the solar system
Unknown-to mans wisdom
Nourishing the eternal light
Marked with uncountable craters
Often bright to guide our sail
Or clipped like a finger nail
Nurtured for eons without fail
Such objects we watch at night
Twinkling with a point of light
Astronomers would make them as charts
Relying on them to unknown parts
Safely guiding us to where we are
Pluto body
Looping orb
Arcing round us
Neptune absorbs
Earth in a celestial-swing
Through the eons it will bring
Saturn, Venus, Jupiters rings

Such a peaceful moment sublime
Only a book-to read and acquire my time
Listening to music soft and mellow
I'm reading a mystery of a mysterious fellow
The dogs asleep by the fire side
Utterly quiet, sleep calls me to bide
Dream of a rural countryside
Enjoying my coffee and reading my paper
Such treasures of time and nuggets to savor

If you could dream of earthly bliss
Man abiding in a world like this
Arms of violence are thrown in the streets
Greeting each other with hugs of peace
It only takes one for the rest to follow
Now is the time to start the succession I guess
Ere you can't have succession without success.

Earth you honor in your flight
Admit to keep goals in obtainable sight
Goals are attainable with persistance and sweat
Lock onto your dreams, they are reachable yet
Engulf the air as winds make you soar
Screech to the sky "I'm chained no more!"

Pluto body
Looping orb
Arcing around us as
Neptune absorbs
Earth in a celestial swing
Through the eons it will bring the stars
Saturn, Venus, Jupiter, Mars

Gardenias on garden shelves
Azaleas sitting by themselves
Red roses strike a customers eyes
Dotted by dainty dragonflies
Each a gardeners prize possession
Now that spring is in full session
Carnations to a gentleman giver
Each hoping a message to deliver
Now I must remember corn and potatoes
Then followed by red ripe sweet tomatoes
Each grown seasonally & to finest perfection
Ready to buy for your selection

Drama, joy, sadness, laughter
Respite from a world is what I'm after
Ebbing from all rush and cares
Awaits an escape from bulls and bears
Markets rise and markets fall
Supervisors expect your call
A moment alone is all your asking
While I'm doing multi-tasking
A cup of coffee with drops of peace
Keep adrift my mind at ease
Enough time seeking the Holy Grail
Now back to business and to sales
I'm feeling better and more empowered
Now I can get back to business fresh
Got a lot more power and a lot more zest

Sprinklers throw a pleasant spray
Upon children who run and play
Muggy heat is chased away
Mudpies is the activity for today
Eyes so soft they beckon you stay
Richness fills this little treasure
Crowning you with so much pleasure
Holding close a gift with no measure
Infinite, timeless, no thief can steal
Locked in your heart security system
Dearness, love, memories, wisdom

Alarm clock rings in morning free dawn
Warm smells of toast and dark coffee (yawn)
Arousing from bed in half drowsed sleep
Keys to find, appointments to keep
Eggs for breakfast and ready to spring
Now let's see, have I forgotten anything?

Dwarfed afar in forests green
Is the soft sound of water running
Soft sounds babbling distant
Trippling rocks in an instant
Afar away I can hear the sound
Not any noise but quiet down
This is such a calming tone
Such like a balming drone
Trees drum at a woodpeckers tapping
Rooting for bugs to be snacking
Eating for a lunchtime meal
Ambling about I see the stream
Moss snuggling on a deep green pine
Solace I drink refreshing my mind.

Ease on back
And enjoy the day
Read tea
Leaves. What do they say?
Get a good cup of tea to steep
Relaxing with a good sleep
Every tension every care
You were given to bear
This is your time you deserve
Each and every day
Aaahmble aaahll your cares aaahway!

My eyes greet the sunlight
Of the new day
Robins are singing
Night had its' play
I wipe my eyes lowly
Now shut off the alarm
Get out of bed slowly and
Brew my joe warm
Rays of sunlit dew drops are
Etched on the grass
And an early morn
Keepsake has found me at last

Rumbles of thunder
Awaken the sky
It shakes me from slumbers
Night lullaby
You feel a calm crystal mist
Near a moonlit spray
It washes and my fears desist
Gently I feel it ebbing away
Hear its' gentle calming mist
To the break of day

Solid drops of water form
Thunder often follows norm
Ominous clouds begin to swell
Raging like a spectre of hell
Malevolent, spiteful skies to dwell

Such a warm quiet day
Lounges a turtle napping away
Eased back in an easy condition
Eased back in a comfortable position
Perhaps he's dreaming of two ice cream scoops
Instead of being turtle soup
Now at rest with eyes asleep
Gnawing his jaw and counting sheep
Tortoises live a very long time
Up to a century in their prime
Rural living they will roam
Traveling in their mobile home
Living on grass, insects by day, napping at night
Enjoying a slow paced leisurely life

You wonder what I'm feeling inside
Oh, if I could only tell
Underneath this shell of pride
Ripens a heart for you to peel
Biding in the first chamber
Eggs a drifting flowing love
And in the second chamber
Undulates my hope from above
Third chamber holds my compassion
Indeed it must flow strong
Fourth chamber holds my passion
Under you it will flow long
Listen to my urgent plea
Life with you is my destiny
Observe the contentment I have for you
Verify you have it too
Evoke the feelings that are true
So rest assured, "I love you"!

Munching on an oven treat
Is a yummy snack to eat
Licking the spoon and the batter
Kreamy smooth is all that matters
With chocolate stirring into a glass
Immerse a white liquid finally at last
Tasting so good an oven fresh bunch
Hungry to eat them for supper and lunch
Crunchy creamy I eat with glee
Or moist and fresh from the bakery
Or watch the baker make a fresh batch
Kneading the mix and make em from scratch
I like to eat them with a glass of cold milk
Even drinking cold that comes from a cow
So much for talking, I'm hungry NOW!

Honeycomb give off an aroma spent
Under its' addictive scent
Now here come a curious bear
Grabbing its' scent in the air
Rich in aroma sifting strong
You just want to follow along
Humming birds find a pine
Oozing liquid runs so fine
Niches hold a honey comb
Each holds a hole a bee calls home
Yellow, sweet and oh so yummy
Bubbly treat for a bears tummy
Eating away without a care
Angry bees are everywhere
Raging, humming, stinging then
Sends the bears back to their den.

Dwarfed aloft two or so miles
Is a world of soft quiet hue
Soaring below clouds of white
Tossed against seas of blue
A song of peace and brotherhood
Nestled in every man
There's a sense it can be achieved
When we stand hand in hand
Hushed in the halls of harmony
Is a voice we all can hear
Stop the gunshots, drugs and hate
Place love inside not fear
Even the most quiet echo
Reverberates like a summer rain
Step one foot ahead and lets' start again

Worlds of jade forest green
Ice capped mountains white
Ninety feet high bove forest streams
Doth the eagle take flight
Now from this height is harmony
Echoing over fields and trees
Alit in its own aerie
Taught never to take more trout than it needs
Hovering over nests it builds
Waves of air again lift it aloft
In natures ever flowing plan
Now again it catches food for its' ever
Growing young
Screeching high harmony a songs need to be sung

Tiny liquid drop of salt
Everyone has them not of fault
A mix of emotions that fill the eyes
Running in portions you can't hide inside

Caressing wick in a section dark
Awaits a taper for a spark
Night encurs and dim impounds
Darkness awaits in flameless rounds
Light awakens a lone dark corner
Encroaching upon it like a foreigner
Lantern glows engulf the room
I can see your loving face
Gracefull walking in this space
Hurry soon to make it glow
Then blow it out before you go

Void of nothing? Not a chance!
Orally in whispers or use them in rants
I won't be quiet to sing my song
Choirs softly, medium or strong
Echoing like angels to the highest clouds aloft
Sing hallelujah, soft to loud to soft

Traveling down this interstate
I'm engulfed in twists of fate
Meandering where does my life go
Ebbing with the tides and flow
With time I will know
If love of mine grows
Then whom shall I choose
How will my heart tell me
Or what will I loose
Untill I fill this void and gap
This voice will sigh and energy sap
Yet on this rock I'll stand strong
Off this rock till you come along
Untill you come along

Tempo or period when something exists
It is our time continuam, not to be missed
Moment, day, week, year
Enjoy these minutes ere they disappear

This day I live
I will be free
My time to give
Equality
Loneliness, but I'm not alone
Embers from my past
Shall soon be thrown
Sunsets finest hour
May still be unknown
Oh never forget in time
Medals await you at the finish line
Each day seize the moment
Never, never ignore it
The time is now
So get out and score it!

Sadness affects me
Tears in my eyes
Anger selects me
Now foolish pride
Don't be ashamed
Blues hits me too
You can't hold inside
You know what to do
Oh, make this love strong
Under this heavy weight
Remember our bond
Strengthened by power
I'll stand by you
Deliver you through
Even in the darkest hour

Comes up the sun
Open your eyes
Moon has descended
Eclipsed by mornin skies
Worship this beautiful day
Heaven opens up its' gift
Adore the songbirds as they sing
The sunrise as it lifts
Every day bring a fresh new morn
Value the good things, not the torn
Enjoy the diary of your life treasures
Rich in newness, keep a measure
May all the ups outweigh the downs
And all the good things be as crowns
Your life be blessed in all you've found

Refreshing as an ocean spray
Anxiety just eases away
In your face a soft blown mist
Nature gives you a nurtured kiss
Sweetened drops on a sultry day
Healed brows are moistened away
Oh, to be under air cooled fans
Water splashing are my plans
Easing away, getting a tan
Rayburns and maybe a fan
Drink an ice cold lemonade
Relaxing with music and a bit of shade
Eventually sleep, no stress or strains
April soon will bring its rains
Must bring in my mattress and my jeans
So now off to bed to finish my dreams

Stashed and hidden is a lot between vines
Each well hoed row not easy-to find
Crops of corn, peas, green beans, tomatoes
Radishes, broccoli, cauliflower, potatoes
Embraced by nature, ready to ripen
Toiled and tilled, ready to happen
Green and fresh salads selectable
Awesomely rich and so delectable
Rapt in mystery, its presence unknown
Draped and cloaked by vines overgrown
Early mornin picked and taken inside and bidden
No one sees this garden that's hidden

Peaceful keys played as angel calls
In minor lifts and major falls
As Eden calls us back to paradise
Notes of music we can't deny
Opus of angels blessed from the skies

Fresh rippling water
On my lips and tongue
Usher in abundance
Neath a burning sun
Trickling love upon me
Overflowing with your grace
Finest time is ahead of us
Bounty is in place
Let your treasures start to rain
Earn my trust like waves of grain
Safely bring me back to home
Save me a stranger as I roam
I ask and plea your abundance give
Now as I raise, in love I live
Glistening streams never ceasing
Sonnets stream, love redeeming

Science, reading, English, Math
Truancy is not a path
A list of subjects, homework, lessons
You'll soon reach your destination
I wonder why to skip classes
Need Ipods? You'll soon need glasses
Sure games on pods an addictive attraction
Classes carry more fun action
Have some fun there and learn some too
Only here can-this come true
Only five days, eight hours of fun I guess
Learn this to be the gameboy of success

Reflection of tears from heavens eyes
Angels weep from clouded skies
Inner hurt, unbearing pain
Numbness to peace, scarcity of prayers
Skies tears to relieve the pain it bears

Come to the party we're holding for you
Everythings ready, there's nothing to do
Lanterns are lit, confetti to throw
Each in a bright festive color to glow
Birthday cake is ready for slicing
Red, white and blue colors for icing
All the games are ready to play
This will be a beautiful day!
Except for you, everyone's here
Laughter, fun, good times and cheer
I've got presents and the rootbeer
For each new day gives gifts to savor
Enjoy this day and party favors!   Wheee!!!

Salty shores on soft sandy beaches
Eyeing the horizon as far as it reachs
As you escape in the emptiness of oceans soft roar
Sea gulls inspire you to come back for more

Recall your life. Where have you been?
Experience your thoughts and bros you've seen
Fall back to the time when you made the scene
Looping in your "mean machine"
Every corner was shined as new
Chamois, chrome and leather too
Tailpipe polished and cragers shined
Im sure to show this car of mine
Or maybe catch some ladys eye
Now rev the motor and make em sigh
Slide on in and cruise around
On a night next to a speaker
Find a lady hot and my car is sleeker
Looking ahead, where's my life going?
I must be planning, must be knowing
For fate is fast, I must prepare
Each one in heaven awaits me there

Ashes from a warmed out fire
Fro and back is it's game
Tossing with ventless desires
Each ever arcing flame
Reaching for a higher flue
Grasping through the smoke
Looking for a reason to imbue
Or to a spark invoke
Warm orange colors still mellow
Gracious red, then orange and yellow
Oh, the colors relaxing hue
Oh, relaxation overdue
Distractions of this in armchair action
Now and then are a pleasant attraction
It's late in the morning
Glowing embers grow low
Here reverie blows silent
The dark room grows cold

Seeping music is my balm
Oozing lifting me to calm
Nightengales over florens
Gently nurse the soul of torrents
Fresh new tune each new day
Orioles are chirping on limbs
Redbirds chirp natures hymns
Alto, soprano, baritone
Nothing matters if we are one
Your voice will blend in harmony
Our pitch will find-that perfect key
Now sing as angels, purr like cats
Eyes sharp, we'll find peace in nothing flat

Expressing from heart the person you were
Lamenting of soul you would never deter
Elevation of others when they have fallen
Grief is relevation when heaven has callen you
You leave our lives better as you sail away. Adieu!

This is my day
I long to live
Moments away
Each morning give
Let me deal with
Each new gain
So to heal to
Start this again
Minute by minute
On this straddling fence
Must enjoy this life and all that's in it
Every motion and sense
Now to be the best I can be this
Taste and experience daily diary
So now share this moment of beauty with me

Silky blue way up high
Kissing you like a lullaby
Yonder clouds pass far and nigh

Capture a moment
Ask yourself
Take time to formulate
Create and delve
Hurrying and waiting
You can't walk away
Our choices debating
Up to this day
Relax in the richness
Balm in its' treasure
Rich in uniqueness
Easing in pleasure
A time out to exhale
This recess of action
Here you have found your holy grail

Before the time you hit the pillow
Eyes would nod, droop and willow
Drifting, but not ready for sleep
Twenty minutes more to keep
I want to hear a tale to tell
Magic and maidens and all that ends well
Each tale you tell, each promise you keep
Sing to me and lull me to sleep
This is the way to get me rest fair
Once upon a time' and-take it from there
Read me a story with a happy ending
I'll fall asleep fast, my dreams I'll be spending
Every night comes tales to ('Yawn') tell
Sleep tight my child, sleep tight and sleep well

Floating gently in a stream
Lifting, moving slow as dreams
Often narrow on skin below
Wrapping readily each gal and fellow

Waves harmonize on an ocean shore
In flight seagulls give an encore
Nothing is heard but a soft sea roar
Gladiolas brimming in springtime bloom
Sunshine brightens-a darkened room
Waltzing with that special one
In the sweet tune of life and all that comes
Twilight echoes in sun colored rains
Harps ping so mellow to comfort our pains
Sitting silent on a quiet afternoon
Tranquility is my pilot, I am landing soon
Rings encircle a star shrouded moon
In the evening the sun is swallowed
Night noise dims o'er all that is hallowed
Great waters fountain every blessing
Sating the thirst with love unceasing

Cardinals singing on a limb
Off away a smoke flue whims
Unique beauty a soft sunbeam bringing
Nestled birds soon start singing
The autumn leaves cover a barn roof
Red birds hover on a limb aloof
Young birds asking from the nest
Colored jays basking get no rest
Alit a cardinal lands with no guilt on
Bright patchwork blocks soft like felt
Intricate designs, blue and red
Nice to land on, feels like bed
Question not why its' draping fence
Up with nature, no escaping hence
Illuminant 'neath an azure sky
Lofts, barns, silos I espy
Trees now bare, white cottage is smokin
Seamed patchwork beauty, my relic, my token

Kinship souls of body and mind
I feel what you feel I'm starting to find
Nature seems to have made us like twins
Down when you lose, up when you win
Rooted from a common tree
Each key like ebony and ivory
Developed in an echoed bond
Such as chessmate and I'am your pawn
Pan the seas broad and shallow
Ignite the candle from its' tallow
Recognize we are as one
In the-evening-and morning sun
The nature within us that we share
So where ever life brings us, I will be there

As I stare at a starry night
I wonder how they glisten so bright
Road maps to stellar destinies
Whispers to my soul in harmony
Atmosphere I breathe on peaceful hills
Violets bloom and daffodils
Exhaling in peace and come it will

As you watch a stary night play
Ink paints your palette blue to gray
Red orange captures a sinking sun
White orb captures a rising moon
Amber grains wave to deep maroon
Violet clouds soon swirl into the haze
Escorting darkness into days thaw
Seeking an asylum point where we can draw

Printed in the United States
By Bookmasters